D0530765

THE
MOST AMAZING
YouTube
DOG
VIDEOS EVER!

First published in Great Britain in 2015 by Prion Books

an imprint of the
Carlton Publishing Group
20 Mortimer Street
London W1T 3JW

A CIP catalogue for this book is available
from the British Library.

ISBN 978-1-85375-942-0

Printed and bound by CPI Group (UK) Ltd, Croydon CR0 4TY

10 9 8 7 6 5 4 3 2 1

THE
MOST AMAZING

DOG

VIDEOS EVER!

THE COOLEST, CRAZIEST AND
FUNNIEST INTERNET DOGGY CLIPS

PRION

INTRODUCTION

This selection of inspired doggy clips from YouTube presents a fabulous glimpse into the canine world. They will have every dog lover laughing, cooing, watching in open-mouthed amazement and occasionally even wiping away a tear.

Having celebrated its tenth birthday in February 2015, YouTube is firmly established as the world's favourite internet site. For the dog lover this is especially true, since our beloved four-legged friends are one of the most popular subjects of uploaded and viewed clips. Some of those dogs featured in this book such as The Mutant Giant Spider Dog, Denver the Guilty Dog, Jiff the Pomeranian and Boo the cutest dog in the world, have even become global stars.

This selection of videos brings together the best of the canine clips on the site. They vary from the adorably sweet to the laugh-out loud funny and from the awesomely talented to the brilliantly bizarre. There are Golden Retrievers, Bulldogs, Great Danes, German Shepherds, Chihuahuas and Spaniels as well as rare pedigree breeds and plenty of plain old mutts. And, of course, you'll find lots and lots of the cutest puppy action!

INAPPROPRIATE LANGUAGE WARNING

The videos selected in this book do not contain any scenes of an explicit sexual or extremely gross nature. However, there is the very occasional use of bad language, which is sometimes part of the video's humour. The comments sections of many of the clips often contain unnecessarily offensive, puerile and abusive language. They rarely feature any remarks of value and are generally worth switching off or ignoring.

DON'T TRY THIS AT HOME

Some of the book's clips feature stunts performed either by professionals or under the supervision of professionals. Accordingly, the publishers must insist that no one attempt to re-create or re-enact any stunt or activity performed on the featured videos.

HOW TO VIEW THE CLIPS

Each entry is accompanied by a QR code, which you can scan with your iPad or iPod. Alternatively, there is a short URL address, which you can type into your own computer, tablet or phone. Unfortunately, many of the clips are preceded by adverts, these can often be skipped after a few seconds, or you may wish to download a reputable advert blocker to prevent them appearing.

CONTENTS

"Why does watching a dog be a dog fill one with happiness."

Jonathan Safran Foer

THE
MOST AMAZING
YouTube
DOG
VIDEOS EVER!

OFF THE LEASH!

Fenton becomes a dog star

Fenton the Labrador became an internet sensation and then a media celebrity when footage of him taken by a 13-year-old hit YouTube in 2012. Fenton was being taken for a walk in Richmond Park in Surrey, England, when he decided to have a little fun chasing the park's famous deer. But what really tickled the nation's funny bone was the increasing panic in the voice of his owner, an architect named Max, as he hopelessly chased Fenton while repeatedly screaming the dog's name interspersed with the odd plaintive cry of "Jesus Christ!"

http://y2u.be/3GRSbr0EYYU

IN THE DOGHOUSE

Someone's helped themselves to the Kitty Cat treats...

This is quite possibly the best whodunnit on the web. We have
incontrovertible evidence found at the crime scene, two suspects
and a detective determined to get to the bottom of the matter.
But who will crack first? Is there a tell-tale sign that they are
the perpetrator of the heinous crime? Will the guilty party give
themselves away? And when the verdict is delivered, will they
accept their punishment without complaint? The famous Denver
the Guilty Dog is worth every one of its 25 million views!

http://y2u.be/B8ISzf2pryl

DOGGY STYLE

An exercise video with a difference – a big difference

There's some really odd stuff on YouTube. Yes, really. It's not uncommon to stumble across somewhat strange, nay bizarre, videos, but this one is just right out there, way past weird and it's somehow important to share it. It's called Poodle Exercise with Humans. We are told that it's a word-for-word parody of a workout video by US celebrity Susan Powter and was made by Japanese pop artist Nagi Noda. However, there's nothing to warn us that it's completely bonkers, totally mesmerizing and could well lead to some disturbing, not to say surreal, nightmares.

http://y2u.be/g8hsl6Y2L-U

"WHAT? YOU ATE ALL THE MEAT IN THE FRIDGE!"

The ultimate dog tease

The Ultimate Dog Tease has been watched by 168 million people, so that probably includes you. However, there is no way we can leave out one of the greatest YouTube videos of all time. This 80-second clip stars a gullible German Shepherd named Clark, who is regaled to slobbering point with the delights of the meat drawer in the fridge — only to be told that they've all been eaten. And if that is hard to take, imagine discovering that the cat has even has been fed some of them. It's too much for a dog to take...

http://y2u.be/nGeKSiCQkPw

BARK SEAT DRIVER

Meet Porter, the world's first driving dog

Porter looks pretty comfortable behind the wheel. It won't be long before he's putting the roof down and driving his pals to the beach. As stunts go, this promotion to prove that rescue dogs are as smart as any other takes some beating. The 10-month-old Bearded Collie had two months of training before being allowed to take the wheel of a specially modified Mini at a racetrack. Amazingly, he is able to start the car, put it into gear and steer the car around the course. Could this herald the end of "walkies" and the dawn of "drivies"?

http://y2u.be/BWAK0J8Uhzk

PRETTY IN PINK

Are you ready for some doggy dress sense?

Do we ever consider how our pets feel when we dress them up?
We might think they look cute, while they are dreading to step
outside of the house for fear of ridicule. If only they could talk...
On the Talking Animal channel they can do just that. Their
cameras caught up with a little Chihuahua in what some might
call an embarrassing shirt. Now the little chap doesn't see it
that way, he's pretty pleased with the little pink number he's
been squeezed into. He's not hearing you snigger and is
ready to give his own opinion on doggy fashion.

http://youtu.be/X8-3Ui0uELU

PUGGY'S GOT IT LICKED

The Pekinese with the longest tongue in the dog world

"He's a silly cartoon-looking dog; that's why I love him." This remark from the owner of Puggy the Pekinese might seem a little harsh on the poor pooch, but he won't mind. Puggy the Pekinese owes a lot to his larger-than-life tongue. When he was a stray, it was his long tongue that got him noticed and once he was cleaned, groomed and loved it won him fame – and a little fortune. At 11.43 centimetres (4.5 inches) long, Puggy's tongue is almost as long as his body. It is the longest canine licker in the world and he has a Guinness record to prove it.

http://youtu.be/BZm3ROACAt0

DAWG! LOOK AT HIM GO!

Tillman – the most famous dog on wheels

In 2009 Tillman the English Bulldog set a world record for the fastest 100 metre canine skateboard, covering the distance in 19.678 seconds. These days, Pot Roast, as he's nicknamed, is a celebrity dog. He's a TV star with his own Facebook page and it really would be no surprise to find him hanging round bus stops in baggy shorts and Vans. Tillman's talents and rise to fame are well chronicled on YouTube. Let's just hope he doesn't get hooked on chews, start paying for visits from bitches and begin endless visits to canine rehab.

http://y2u.be/CQzUsTFqtW0

OLD DOG, NEW TRICKS

He's not called Jumpy for nothing...

This four-and-a-half-year-old Border Collie could just be the most talented mutt in the world. OK, he does the expected – the back-flipping Frisbee-catching, the surfing, the skateboarding and the slalom-running – but Jumpy has a whole host in his repertoire, some of them simply incredible. Just watch him go! And he can do charming, too. Indeed, with a wink and a modest paw over his face, Jumpy appears to be a better actor than many of his human Hollywood counterparts. Want to see more of Jumpy? Search for *Bad Ass Dog 2+*.

http://y2u.be/5I_QzPLEjM4

ON HIS TROLLEY

Taking a luxury ride

Next time you visit your local supermarket and wonder what's happened to all the trolleys, here's your answer. The local pooches are using them as mobility carts. Watch here as Maymo the Lemon Beagle pushes his puppy sister Penny through the town to the playground. All very cute, but it raises some serious questions. Where would a dog get the token or coin to release the trolley in the first place? Couldn't they do something more useful, like get the weekly shopping? And who is carrying the little plastic bags for their "gifts"?

http://y2u.be/cVg2QEYtdIM

CUTEST DOG ON THE PLANET

Meet Boo the dog – he's too cute!

"My name is Boo. I am a dog. Life is Good" is how this Pomeranian launched his journey to fame. He is now an internet sensation with 10 million Facebook likes, his own publications, a job as Virgin America's "spokesdog" and an endorsement by Khloe Kardashian, who says he is indeed the "cutest dog on the planet". So here's your chance to see what all the fuss is about. Boo being shy, Boo dressed up, Boo playing with a soft toy. It's nothing any old mongrel hound couldn't do, but there's no denying it, this dog is darned cute.

http://y2u.be/peKSCssJTqE

DEMON DOG

Staines gets psyched by cupcakes

Anyone who's seen the iconic *Dramatic Chipmunk* YouTube clip will know where this one is heading. It features Staines, an Australian Shepherd dog, who is appearing on a TV dog training show. For the discipline test, the dog is presented with a plateful of cupcakes and must retain its self-control. As the strain begins to show, it seems that the only way Staines will get through it is to enter a zen-like trance...

http://y2u.be/t-XIMEHGoZI

COMPLETELY BARKING

Weird dog with an even weirder bark

This is the dog's chops – a fantastic gabbling Poodle-cross that sounds as weird as it looks. You might be tempted to wonder just what it's talking about, but I really wouldn't bother. If you did manage to translate the strange yelpings, they'd probably be the equivalent of that strange bloke at the bus stop screaming, "The cucumbers are coming to get us. Guard your rawlplugs!" But if you enjoy this – and you will – be sure to check out *Videoresponse to The Weirdest Dog Ever,* then explain what that's all about!

http://y2u.be/LNqeZVL_ZHE

MUTT WITH THE MOVES

For those who like their sport with a side dish of culture

Here's Nathan, whipping his hair back and forth, and moving like he was born on the dance floor. Pharrell Williams' hit song 'Happy' was everywhere in 2014 and was just crying out for someone to have a viral hit. So step forward, Nathan, possibly the ugliest dog in the world, for a well-earned five minutes of fame. And it couldn't be a lovelier story. Nathan was a rescue dog with quite a sad past, but by the look of things he's settled down pretty well in his new home!

http://y2u.be/x_wgb1q1opQ

MAN'S BEST FRIEND

If people were pets

This very funny film considers who makes for the better human companion – the over-affectionate hound or the indifferent mog? Fatawesome's unique spin is that they ask what life would be like if your mates acted like your pets. How would you cope with someone who greeted you like a long-lost friend when you'd only been out for five minutes? Or how would you feel about your buddy waking you up in the middle of the night because he fancied some cereal? They've also made an amusing sequel showing just how these pet "friends" can really mess up your life.

http://y2u.be/GbycvPwr1Wg

DOGS' DINNER

Join Nono and Sia on a posh dinner date

"Hey, Sia, where are you having dinner tonight?"
"Same as ever – in the corner of the kitchen,
right where they keep my bowl."
"Fancy something a little different?"
"Have you been stealing from the bin again, Nono?"
"No. I just thought we might go out."
"This isn't leading up to your Nandogs or McDogalds
joke again, is it?"
"No dawg! Get your best jumper on – we're going upmarket..."

http://y2u.be/EVwlMVYqMu4

MUTANT GIANT SPIDER DOG

Mayhem on the streets as the spider dog goes on the rampage

It looks real enough. And terrifying enough. A giant mutant spider is roaming the streets, chasing its victims into the enormous webs it has built. But this is the brilliant work of Polish YouTuber Sylwester Wardega. He has dressed his dog Chica in a spider costume, let him loose in the local streets, and filmed the ensuing mayhem. People going about their lives are naturally scared out of their wits and even more frightened as they come across the rope webs that Sylwester has rigged up, complete with fake human remains. His reward for such imagination was to earn the Number 1 "top trending video" of 2014.

http://y2u.be/YoB8t0B4jx4

THE DOG TEASER

Magician uses disappearing dog treats as the ultimate dog tease

We've all had fun teasing our four-legged friends, even if it's just pretending to throw a stick and watching them scurry off towards the horizon. Magician Jose Ahonen is a dog teaser in a class of his own. He offers them a dog treat under their very noses, but before they get a chance to snap it up, he makes it vanish. The dogs' reactions are priceless. Desperately looking around, even nature's own detectives are bemused and befuddled by a sleight of hand. Dog lovers can rest easy: we are assured that all participants were soon rewarded with enough treats to compensate.

http://y2u.be/VEQXeLjY9ak

DOGGY STYLE

A high-energy, dog's-eye view of a dash to the beach

The high definition, lightweight GoPro camera has provided a number of YouTube hits from extreme sports feats to stalking sharks. "Run Walter, RUN!" is one of the latest of them to go viral. It features a labrador harnessed with a GoPro camera to capture a dog's eye view. On a scorching day in Siracusa, Sicily, Walter is let off his leash. He runs from the house with only one aim – to get to the sea as quick as possible. Within 30 seconds Walter has cleared gates, steps, rocks and bemused sunbathers on the beach to plunge into the Mediterranean for a refreshing swim.

http://y2u.be/UowkIRSDHfs

DOG BLASTS HORN

Impatient hound takes the wheel — and the horn

When Fern the Boxer got left in the car on her own for too long, she found the ideal way to make her owners pay. Show them up on YouTube! The 18-month-old dog had been left in the car while her owner took in an art gallery in Broughty Ferry, near Dundee in Scotland. Fern was clever enough to know that simply barking at passers-by would not help matters at all, so she climbed in the driver's seat, leaned back and sounded the horn with her paw — repeatedly. Two million views online? That'll teach him not to leave me again!

http://y2u.be/y3xEPpwWGqk

LET IT HOWL

Puppy's amazing response to the hit from *Frozen*

We all know that little girls love the film *Frozen* and adore its song 'Let It Go'. But who knew it was a big hit in the pet world too? Here's Oakley, the cutest Australian Shepherd puppy. He's enjoying his nap despite Charli XCX's 'Boom Clap' blaring out of the car speakers. Then, on comes 'Let it Go' and Oakley's little ears perk up. In moments he's up and ready for action, which in his case means howling along to his favourite song. When the track is switched again, Oakley's not interested. He's ready to settle back and dream of his life with Princess Anna.

http://y2u.be/ezz2NqvlORY

MUNCHKIN WORKS OUT

It's walkies time for adorable Munchkin, the Teddy Bear Shih Tzu

Now you might find this adorable or you might just think things have gone way too far. Munchkin is a Shih Tzu from South California. She is pretty sweet as it is, but dressed up in her Teddy Bear outfit, and appearing to walk standing up, she pushes the cuteness into the red zone. Munchkin the Teddy Bear made her name as an Instagram sensation but found no problem transferring her skills to YouTube. Here she is working out on the treadmill, and you can also find videos of her on the red carpet, on the beach and out sleighing.

http://y2u.be/mVmBL8B-In0

A MAN'S BEST FRIEND IS HIS ROBODOG

Introducing Spot, the electric-powered robot dog

You may have already seen BigDog, a gas-powered robot dog from the Boston Dynamic company. Now he has a little friend named Spot, who is electric-powered with a sensor head and super hydraulics. The 72-kilo (160-pound) robot dog isn't the cutest mutt you've ever come across, but it can canter along next to a human, climb stairs and walk off-road. It can keep its balance when the meanest of people take a kick at it and most impressively, it can walk next to BigDog without succumbing to the urge to sniff its bottom.

http://y2u.be/M8YjvHYbZ9w

IN THE DOGHOUSE – AGAIN

Denver the Guilty Dog is back in a Christmas confessional

It's the return of the brilliant Denver the Guilty Dog! In an earlier entry, we watched the adorable yellow Labrador facing up to having devoured a bag of cat treats. Thankfully, he's been caught in the act again. This time Denver – in collaboration with the cat – has been feeding on the foam ornaments from the Christmas tree. The red dye around the dog's mouth is a dead giveaway, but poor Denver gives that look that says, "Okay you got me! I did it. I'm weak and naughty. Please, please forgive me." And who wouldn't?

http://y2u.be/ogZWYn6qHSk

SMART-HOUND BUS

It's a smart dog that knows its own way to the park — by bus!

Passengers on a Seattle bus have grown used to seeing an
unaccompanied dog taking up one of the seats. It roams the
aisles looking for a spare seat, hops up and happily sits looking
out the window. When the bus reaches the park, he gets up and
waits for the doors to open. The owner of the dog is usually a
bus or two behind, having waited to finish his cigarette. Eclipse
is a Black Labrador/Bullmastiff cross and seems to charm all
the passengers he meets on the bus.

http://y2u.be/Bz4XEpK6INU

CANINE CUDDLE

A distressed dog is comforted by his canine pal in this feelgood clip

---

What would be happening in a dog's nightmare? Do they dream of zombie dogs on the rampage? Failing their test at the obedience class? Or something as simple as the family getting a new cat? Jackson, a pretty wonderful-looking one-year-old Double Doodle (the poster says that's half Goldendoodle and half Labradoodle) is having a bad dream involving a lot of scurrying actions. Fortunately, help is at hand in the form of his canine friend Laika. Her reaction to her young pal's discomfort is heart-warming. As one comment says, we all need a Laika in our lives.

http://y2u.be/uTy_wUkWpkM

A REAL LIFE-SAVER

Dog to the rescue in not near-drowning accident

This dog is never off duty. Despite reclining on the river bank, he's got an eye on his human friend who is having a dip on the river. And the watchful canine fears the worst when he sees the swimmer's head dip underwater. He jumps straight into the river and lands right on his owner's head. He's not finished yet. Grabbing the man's hand in his mouth, he starts paddling away and pulling him back to shore. Although the swimmer was fine all along, it's reassuring to know his best pal was looking out for him.

http://y2u.be/dSF8B45AcDw

POCKET-SIZED POOCH

Heaven Sent Brandy, the world's smallest dog

Like many dogs Heaven Sent Brandy, the Chihuahua from Florida, USA is not allowed on the furniture. In her case, it's because if she jumps off, she'd break a bone. Measuring just 15.2 centimetres (6 inches) from tail to nose, the adorable four-year-old is no bigger than a can of cola and is the world's smallest dog in terms of length. She's a nervous little creature – but who can blame her, when every hulking great human in sight wants to cuddle her?

http://y2u.be/fTEIdAyYkac

SURF'S PUP

Abbie Girl, the incredible surfing dog

Abbie Girl, an Australian Kelpie, is a rescue dog with a rags to riches story. Needing rehabilitation for trauma, Abbie Girl was taken to the beach by her adopted owner, Michael Uy, in order to develop her self-confidence. She immediately took to surfing on both boogie boards and long boards. Soon she became the world's greatest surfing dog, riding breaks nearly 1.8 metres (6 feet) high and setting a the record for the longest wave surfed by a dog at 59 metres (65 yards).

http://y2u.be/FJqS2vZMakl

A TWO-LEGGED FRIEND

The most famous dog in the world?

His Facebook page has over 14 million likes, he has over 850,000 followers on Instagram and he numbers pop princess Katy Perry amongst his friends. Jiff the pint-sized Pomeranian from Los Angeles has got to be the most famous dog in the world. Of course it helps that he is as cute as a button, especially when dressed up, but Jiff is also a talented pooch: he is the world's fastest dog on both his hind legs and on his front legs.

http://y2u.be/5CaDC-ou7kg

PUPPY LOVE

Do you take this poodle..?

It was the wedding of the year, a lavish $200,000 ceremony organized by a celebrity wedding planner. The bride wore a spectacular gown valued at $6,000, while the groom was attired in a designer tuxedo. For this was the most expensive pet wedding in history — a charity event that saw Baby Hope, a Coton de Tulear puppy, marry Chilly Pasternak, a Poodle. The event was even officiated by a celebrity pet in Triumph, the Insult Comic Dog, well-known on American TV.

http://y2u.be/t_Q9c_r5MuY

UGLY MUTT

Every dog is beautiful. Except maybe...

Two-year-old Peanut, a mutt who is suspected of being a Chihuahua/Shitzu mix, doesn't have a lot going for him. He was seriously burned as a puppy and lived in an animal shelter for nine months before he found a home. On the looks side he has matted hair, protruding teeth and looks as much rodent as canine. However, in California in 2014, Peanut found fame. In a hotly contested competition, he swept the floor with the other hideous hounds and was crowned "The World's Ugliest Dog".

http://y2u.be/7AkYSGIlKTk

DOG ON WHEELS

It's Norman the Scooter Dog

He's a three-year-old French Sheepdog with a special talent. Ever since he was a puppy, Norman has been climbing on board a scooter and propelling himself along. Norman balances himself on the scooter with his two front paws on the handle and a back paw on the scooter. He uses his other hind paw to push himself forward. Having already earned the moniker Norman the Scooter Dog, he then scooted 100 metres in just over 20 seconds – a world record for a dog on a scooter!

http://y2u.be/qKYryJ_1poQ

WARM WELCOME

A heart-warming compilation of dogs welcoming soldiers home

How much would your dog miss you if you went away for months on end? Probably just as much as these creatures miss their owners who have been away on military duty. Big or small, fighters or toy dogs, they share a boundless excitement about welcoming a friend back into their lives. The compilation featuring dogs welcoming US soldiers home is ridiculously heart-warming. It's fascinating to watch the dogs' reaction when they recognize the soldiers and how they completely lose themselves in the excitement of the moment.

http://y2u.be/eZ6oS5dUT30

DOG ON THE DECKS

The DJ dog gets right in the groove

Most dogs like a good scratch from time to time, but French bulldog DJ Mama isn't getting her claws out to an itch behind the ear — she's scratching out a beat on vinyl. Her owner, DJ Greyboy, always had her at his feet when he was on the decks and it seems Mama picked up some skills. When he let her get her paws on the turntable, he discovered she had a talent as a DJ. She instantly picked up a rhythm and scratched along note for note with DJ Greyboy.

http://y2u.be/6zMJ8o6UWD0

BATHTIME!

Some dogs will do anything to avoid having a bath

"So I pong a bit, what's the problem with that?" Bathtime is just not at the top of their list of leisure opportunities. For any young dog wondering just how they might avoid it, this video acts as a useful tutorial. Running away is for novices, they are just going to catch you. Hiding under the bed is a better idea — or how about turning vicious and see if you can delay the inevitable that way? Others favour burying themselves in the sofa or even clinging onto the walls. And remember, never give up, you can always desperately suspend yourself above the water line...

http://youtu.be/V4LnorVVxfw

IT'S ONLY A CAT!

When you're just too scared to walk past a cat

"I'm not going to come up there and get you," exclaims an exasperated owner on this compilation. "You've got to learn to walk past a cat." These poor dogs. They are expected to be fearless; brave ancestors of hunting animals whose very bark puts the fear of God into any other creature. Yet they find themselves unable to summon the courage to pass a brooding, inscrutable feline presence who for some reason sits nonchalantly in the middle of the stairs. It's enough to give a poor mutt an inferiority complex.

http://youtu.be/WNkb44o1NWA

PUPPY DREAMS

A too-cute-for-words puppy talking in his sleep

We're heading into the cuteness red zone with this clip. It's a nine-day-old Shiba Ina puppy with a sweet little doll – and it's talking (or, more accurately, squeaking) in its sleep. Shiba Inu are a Japanese breed – "Inu" meaning "dog" – in Japanese and they are nicknamed the Little Brushwood Dog. They are a favourite breed in Japan and their puppies are indescribably adorable. So what could this darling little fella dreaming about? Rainbows? Unicorns jumping on fluffy clouds? Or perhaps, he's heading out on a ninja adventure?

http://youtu.be/-klJqXLMLwc

A HELPING HOUND

When it comes to household chores, every home needs a Jesse...

Fetching a ball, playing dead, shaking hands – those tricks are fine, but in this busy modern world we need a dog who can offer more. So, meet Jesse, he doesn't perform tricks; he does chores! This fabulous Jack Russell Terrier likes nothing better than to lend a helping paw around the house. He wipes down the worktops, cleans the windows and even puts his bowl in the dishwasher. When you get home he unties your shoes and takes your socks off and puts them in the washing machine, before coming back to give you a massage. What a dog!

http://youtu.be/P9Fyey4D5hg

JUST WANTS TO NAP!

A puppy who really wants a nap

This little Bichon Frisé puppy might remind you of being in class in that long afternoon maths lesson when every inch of you wants to fall asleep but you know you can't. Keeping your eyes open is a test of strength and your mind has already set off for the land of nod. So here's the cutest of puppies fighting the urge as her eyelids get heavier and heavier. She's telling herself that perhaps something really exciting might be about to happen. And then it starts – the head drops, the eyes close, but she's still standing. Just...

http://youtu.be/YZlFiF4Zuys

MISHKA, THE TALKING DOG

The dog that says "I love you" – and more...

Introducing Mishka, the internet's favourite talking dog (who also happens to have gorgeous eyes!). The Siberian Husky's videos have been viewed millions of times, she has been on TV and has her own Facebook and Instragram accounts. Among the phrases she has picked up are "Hello", "How are you?" and "I'm hungry" – some uttered a little more clearly than others. But there is no doubting that Mishka's clearest and most endearing attempt at speech is saying "I love you" in her doggy accent. If you want to hear more – including Mishka singing 'Jingle Bells' – there's plenty more in the gardea23 account.

http://youtu.be/2c8MMiytwNs

SLEEP SPRINTING

Bizkit, the sleepwalking dog, goes viral

With over 30 million views poor Bizket has become a bit of a laughing stock on YouTube. This lovely Golden Labrador was filmed while enjoying a well-earned nap. Bizket, however, wasn't getting a lot of rest, as she was living every minute of her dream. At first she is padding along and then develops into a full-on sleep sprint. Bizket is totally immersed in her dream, so much so that even when she gets up she is still in the chase. What happens next is simply hilarious...

http://youtu.be/z2BgjH_CtlA

HERO DOG

A dog saves his dog friend on a busy motorway

The CCTV surveillance film of a motorway picked out the amazing heroics of a dog in Santiago, Chile. Although the footage is low quality and some of the scenes are a little upsetting, it is an incredibly heart-warming story. First we see a poor dog attempting to cross the busy road and being left for dead after being hit by a truck. Shortly afterwards another dog appears on the film. Showing incredible heroism, it braves the frightening traffic and pulls the injured dog to the safety of the side of the road, where it is attended to by road workers.

http://youtu.be/OctjlROdNcc

AN ILL WIND...

It's a Pug who is terrified of a fart

The dog world doesn't share the human obsession with the fart. They don't find the noisy expulsion of a little bottom wind anything to be embarrassed about, giggle about or be ashamed of. When his owner lets one rip, though, this little pug jumps out of his skin. The poster explains that the pug was from a rescue home having had a tough life, including losing his tail. Perhaps that is why the dog is so nervous. Still, we are laughing with him, not at him – and it is pretty funny!

http://y2u.be/S06dcExPgno

TIGER ADOPTION

Tally the dog adopts three tiger cubs

When a tiger at the Oktyabrsky Zoo in the Black Sea resort of Sochi in Russia abandoned her cubs, an urgent appeal was put out on the internet for a feeding surrogate mother. No nursing tiger could be found, but a white Swiss Shepherd dog stepped into the breach to save the cubs. Although the cubs at first bared their claws and hissed at their new mother, Tally proved a patient parent. Nursing and caring for the baby tigers as if they were her own, she soon won their affection.

http://youtu.be/ZmyKyEfx3Ng

TAKE IT AWAY, TUCKER...

A tune from a piano-playing Schnoodle

After receiving complaints from their neighbours about strange noises when they left the house, a family set up a video camera to get to the bottom of the mystery. What they discovered was that Tucker, their one-and-a-half-year-old Schnoodle, had been secretly practising playing the piano. Tucker gets up on the stool, studies the sheet music and sings along as he tinkers the ivories. The post tells us that he now practises at least three or four times every day, then admits, "he really isn't getting any better at it."

http://youtu.be/PiblYasnzWE

YOU'VE GOT TO BE KIDDING!

A Great Dane can't believe the size of his bed

This is just a video of a huge dog and a small bed. It's clear from the very start that it's just too tiny. Simple maths say a Great Dane into a Dachshund-sized bed won't go. But this big fella isn't going to give up that easy. He gives it a good inspection, tries the sides to see if they might extend and views it from every side. Only when he's completely sure that, yep, it doesn't get any bigger, does he plonk his backside down with the smallest of defeated sighs.

http://youtu.be/JQGC3ppdP3k

I'M TELLING ON YOU

**Can a desperate show of affection prevent
Lilo getting a telling off?**

"I'm going to tell your dad when he gets home … He's going
to be not happy with you." Lilo has been caught red-pawed
chewing up her brand new pet bed. Her only chance is that her
owner's roommate, who caught her in the act, won't spill the
beans when he gets home. Thinking fast, Lilo goes for a
charm offensive – cuddling up to him and licking him on the
nose. Is her plan going work? Judging by the knowing
smile he gives the camera, I don't think so.

http://youtu.be/0FK3mxoMXJc

HOME ALONE

**Ever wondered what your dog does
when you leave the house?**

Oh no! You might never leave your dog alone again after
watching this video. YouTube user Mike The Intern attached
a GoPro camera to his dog's collar and recorded what happens
after he left the house. The result was heart-wrenching.
The dog repeatedly and desperately checks the door and
looks out the window for Mike – he can't have just gone, he
seems to be thinking. Then it finally dawns on him that he
really has been left alone... watch the three-and-a-half
minutes through, but be prepared to shed a tear.

http://youtu.be/O_J-XwrYSzw

HOME ALONE – VERSION 2

"And remember, no getting on the bed while I'm out..."

Of course, there are less sentimental reasons for not
leaving your mutt alone in the house... This dog is not allowed
on the bed (unlike the cat who sits there imperiously),
so a suspicious owner sets up a camera to see just what
it gets up to when she leaves home. No whining or crying for
this guy; a quick check that she's gone and he's up, rolling on
as much as that bed as he can. And while, he's there,
he might as well try and shove that smug cat off too!

http://youtu.be/7D5bPLxU8U8

PIT BULL MEETS ITS NEMESIS

Why is this Pit bull frightened to enter the kitchen?

The Pit bull is one of the most misunderstood dogs on the planet. Thanks to some irresponsible owners and some sensationalist newspaper stories, many believe them to be naturally aggressive and vicious fighting dogs. Fortunately, some Pit bulls, like Stella in this video, are doing their best to destroy the stereotype. Stella is in the kitchen, but something is worrying her. When her owner brings it a little closer, Stella is visibly scared. What is it? Only a pineapple! Check out the clip called *Pitt bull is no longer terrified of pineapple* to see Stella overcome her fears.

http://youtu.be/cR3SvL2SmDo

GROWING UP FAST

Charting a dog's growth from puppy to full-grown adult

Sophia (also known as Diablo's Tuscan Dream) is a Rhodesian Ridgeback, and this beautiful time-lapse film show the changes as she grows from a puppy into a magnificent full-sized adult. YouTuber Greg Coffin took a picture of Sophia in the same pose and in the same spot in the house regularly from when she first came into their lives as a two-month-old puppy until she develops into a beautiful three-year-old. As the time-lapse film runs we can watch the progression in just 23 seconds — and then watch it all backwards!

http://youtu.be/c6eUidLqUAo

FETCH FAILS

A compilation of dogs doing what they do best, badly

Catching and fetching? That's supposed to be a dog's *raison d'être*, isn't it? The activity that makes their whole life worthwhile. Well, that and the butt-sniffing. They are meant to be super-skilled at catching objects mid-air or, failing that, chasing them down quickly, whether they are dog treats, balls or frisbees. So it's great to see them failing at the simplest of fetching feats — and even better to watch it in slow motion. No wonder that this two-minute compilation of un-coordinated, short-sighted, misjudging, over-eager or, best-of-all, completely uninterested mutts has had over two million views.

http://youtu.be/ltSOG7KA7XQ

A HELPING HOUND

A flooded street brings out the best in a four-legged friend

If you have any doubt at all that a dog is a man's best friend, just watch this 30-second clip. It is a film taken by a mobile phone through a car window as it slowly drives along a flooded Russian street. Although the footage is low quality, the amazing sight they witness is clear to see. A man in a wheelchair is being pushed through the knee-high water by a dog walking on his hind legs. The story behind the footage remains a mystery, but thanks to the clip going viral, the unknown dog is now a hero around the world.

http://youtu.be/00GozdnJLTQ

HEY! THAT'S MY BED

A puppy is determined to get his bed back

Being sweet doesn't hold much sway with a cat. Pixel is a 10-week-old French Bulldog and as cute as a button. He's a little upset that the family cat has stolen his bed and doesn't look like giving it back. Ten weeks isn't a lot of time to learn the strategies of getting round a pesky cat, so poor old Pixel does what he can to get his bed back. A lot of tugging and some posturing before running away isn't going to shift this cat. Indeed, she looks thoroughly unimpressed.

http://youtu.be/ssC1JDCXk2M

INVISIBLE FORCE FIELD

What's stopping this Terrier from joining the fun?

Outside the terrace doors stands a sweet little Terrier waiting to join the fun inside. The family call and call him to get him to come in, but something is preventing him from entering the house. Although the door is open, it seems there is a force field stopping him. Perhaps he's run into too many glass doors in the past and has decided you can't be too careful. Is there any end to this madness? Will someone have to pick him up and carry him through the open door? Then one of the guests comes up with the perfect, and hilarious, solution...

http://youtu.be/udbMNZDQS48

FACE THE FEAR

Rocky the French Bulldog puppy learns to jump

Hey! What d'you want? I was just settling to a nice little nap.
No, I'm fine, thanks, already had some dinner. You want me to jump?
Into your arms? No way. You're like a whole two feet away. You're
not going to leave me alone are you? OK, I'll give it a go. One,
two, three... nah. On second thoughts, I like napping best. If I
do it once, will you leave me alone? Here goes... Geronimo! Wow!
That was great. Can we do it again?

http://y2u.be/-n4XX5nnXhU

CRIMINAL MASTERMIND

Secret cameras catch Lucy the sneaky Beagle in the act

More home alone antics, but this time the kitchen is the crime scene under surveillance. Lucy the Beagle is suspected of being up to no good when left to fend for herself. How will the video evidence look in court? Well, Lucy has a quick scout around under the dinner table, that's no crime. And, we can forgive her for getting up on the table for a sniff and a lick. However, when she notices something cooking in the toaster oven, Lucy's ingenious criminal mind goes to work... Guilty as charged, M'lud.

http://youtu.be/_ym0rxis0pw

FASTEST DOG ON TWO LEGS

Two-legged inspiration Duncan Lou Who goes to the beach

At first, this looks like a normal puppy enjoying every moment of his first trip to the beach. But you soon notice the cute Boxer puppy has only his front legs. This is Duncan Lou Who, who first captured hearts when he appeared on YouTube in an inspiring story of how he recovered after having his severely deformed hind legs amputated. This subsequent video shows the now nine-month-old Duncan having a ball on Rockaway Beach in New York. Having abandoned his wheelchair, Duncan displays perfect balance as he runs and plays with his doggy and human friends.

http://youtu.be/xaM-xXgl4Bs

BUSKING DOG

A singing street dog accompanies a busker

Who knows how much Ukrainian street musician Sergei Ivanovich usually picks up when he's playing solo, but when the clarinettist is joined by a singing stray dog, there are plenty of coins being thrown in his hat. Sergei claims not to have seen the dog before it joined him in this clip, but the singer seems familiar enough with the tunes. Indeed, the dog's howls sound more tuneful than the clarinet. Apparently spectators begged the musician to adopt the singer, but he declined, saying he already had a dog at home. The pooch probably has another gig to go to anyway.

http://youtu.be/Tl8ojv2K7h0

FATHER'S DAY

English Bulldog father meets his daughter for the first time

Almost 10 million people have viewed this adorable five-minute clip of a English Bulldog meeting his puppy daughter for the first time. While the young dog gets busy doing what puppies do, it is the reaction of Dad that pulls you in. At first, he seems bemused at the arrival of this "mini me", wondering just who she is and why she thinks she can play with his bone treat. Soon enough, however, that father-daughter bond kicks in and the two start playing together. And, even when he, hilariously, gets up to leave, he then decides to stay for one last little game. A simply adorable video.

http://youtu.be/nN7YWz2RqH8

CLUB WOOF!

Classy music video with a canine twist

Let me take you to this really cool bar, where the music's smooth and the clientele beautiful. The twist? How about the fact that the only man in here is the ruggedly handsome singer... other than him, it's wall to wall glamorous women and, you've guessed it, dogs! This video for Mayer Hawthorne's hit 'Her Favorite Song' features this fabulous fantasy canine club, where the house band is made up of jazz dogs in hats and shades, the DJ is a Basset Hound with headphones, the barmen are tuxedoed mutts and even the drunks are dogs!

http://youtu.be/RWkjcq_N2YQ

SWIMMING WITH DOLPHINS

Maverick by name, maverick by nature!

Tourists around the world pay good money to go swimming with dolphins, so why shouldn't dogs? Maverick, a German Shepherd, was intrigued when he spotted dolphins alongside his fishing boat. After watching their games for a few seconds, he just had to join them. A leap and a splash and he was ready to play. Unsurprisingly, Maverick's fish friends disappeared pretty quickly and he was left swimming alone in the big ocean. Never mind, he's a strong swimmer and is soon hauled back to safety — with a video of his big adventure to watch later.

http://youtu.be/IP5Gaticbc4

JUST SAY "NO"

Blaze doesn't want to go in his kennel

This clip is called *Blaze Loves His Kennel*, but that doesn't appear to be the case. Talking dog Blaze, an 11-month-old Husky, has learned only one human word, but it's the only one he needs. They want him to go to his kennel, but Blaze is perfectly happy drifting off to sleep on the floor. Though they ask him nicely — again and again — Blaze has his answer ready, every time. When his owner asks him for the umpteenth time to go to his kennel, you are half expecting Blaze to reply, "What part of 'no' don't you understand?"

http://youtu.be/hCRDskZrUMU

WEIRD AND WEIRDER

Celebrating the weird relationship of a dog and its owner

The things you say and do with your pooch may not seem odd at the time, but when you stop and think about it, they might look pretty strange to others. In this amusing video Eugene Lee Yang and his adorable puppy Pesto show just how weird the dog-owner relationship can get. Surely every loving dog owner has found themselves pleading, "Poop, Poop for me", pretending to taste "yummy" dog food or desperately googling which foods their canine pal can eat? Go on, admit it, you've done all these and much, much more...

http://youtu.be/7Y_Ldy5avWM

DOGS CAN FLY

Introducing Vhobe, the Dock Jumping champion

Dock jumping is a fast-growing event that is pulling in crowds across the world. It requires the dog to run down the dock (a wooden jetty) at full pace and, encouraged by their handlers, leap as far as they can into the water. Five-year-old Vhoebe du Loups du Soleil (they call her V-Bee) is a Belgian Malinois from San Diego, California. A living legend in the dock jumping world, she is a world champion and the world record holder with a jump of over 9 metres (30 feet) – nearly as long as a double-decker bus!

http://youtu.be/KTx64Z4-x9M

WATERMELON TORTURE

The hilarious teasing of a polite Pomeranian

The beguiling Pomeranian only wants a piece of watermelon.
As his owner brings a chunk of the fruit to his lips, the dog is
transfixed just imagining the taste. However, as the owner glances
in his direction, the fluffy white dog quickly looks away. It's funny
the first time he does it, funnier the second and hilarious the third
fourth and fifth times. By the end you'll either be saying, "Go on,
give the dog a chunk" or "Please, one more time". This brilliant
clip from Korea has been viewed over a million times.

http://youtu.be/ERvbs3UjHVU

AMELIA KNOWS THE ANSWER

Hands up if you've seen this clip before?

Get ready for an eight-second canine clip that is 100% guaranteed to make you smile. The star of the show, Amelia, a five-year-old Brittany Spaniel, is having a well-deserved Sunday morning lie-in. It is not a time for jumping around, learning new tricks or running excitedly about like a puppy. In fact, it's all Amelia can do to keep her eyes open. So when she's asked, "Who's the best dog in the world?", she gives her answer in the most effortless way possible. And gets the only appropriate reply.

http://youtu.be/PsLm6_qHeag

BIG EARS

Meet Harbor, a Coonhound with the longest ears in the world

When Harbor was a puppy, his ears were so long he would trip over them and fall down the stairs. But now he is the ripe old age of eight, those very ears have made him a celebrity in his hometown of Boulder, Colorado. For Harbor, a black and tan Coonhound, has the longest ears of any dog in the world! His left ear is 31.1 centimetres (12.25 inches) long, while his right ear is even longer, at 34.3 centimetres (13.5 inches). Harbor is no freak, though: Coonhounds as a breed have long ears to aid their excellent sense of scent.

http://youtu.be/MV0_LsYT9xY

IT'S NOT THE WINNING THAT COUNTS

Golden Retriever mistakes race for a picnic

It is one of the toughest rounds in *Koira Mestari* (which loosely translates as "dog champion"), the Finnish version of Crufts that tests a dog's obedience, concentration and speed. Competing dogs are required to run a short course ignoring the meat, treats, balls and toys that have been placed to tempt them into halting their sprint. The dogs are amazing in their focus, ignoring the distractions and heading directly for the finish. All except one. As this Golden Retriever set off on the course, the idea of winning the competition was suddenly the last thing on his mind...

http://youtu.be/5iTTNRE-njM

ULTIMATE FETCH

The world record frisbee chase and catch

Rob McLeod and Davy Whippet are record breakers. Before they met, Rob was a champion frisbee thrower while young pup Davy showed signs of being a fast chaser. When Davy's owner brought them together, something magical happened. After a few practice competitions, they went for the big one – the world record. As Rob launches the frisbee, Davy sets off. The Whippet reaches 64km/h (40mph) as he careers across the field, arriving with perfect timing to launch himself and snare the disc. He had run 123 metres (402 feet) in just 10.56 seconds, beating a record that stood for 18 years.

Http://youtu.be/aCeBkn7hjbM

THE BALANCING QUEEN OF ILLINOIS

A dog with an unusual record...

Sweet Pea from Illinois, USA is one talented dog. The Border Collie–Australian Shepherd cross spends around three hours a day practising her balancing acts. This video show the first time she walked up stairs blindfolded while balancing a glass of water on her nose. I mean to say, how on earth do you start to teach a dog to do that? Since then she has gone on to star on German TV and break the record for the fastest 100 metres with a can balanced on her head.

http://youtu.be/68PMF7Xxppl

TRACTOR PULL

Is this the strongest dog in the world?

Kangal dogs are a Turkish breed similar to a Mastiff. They are
used in shepherding, not to herd the flock but to act as guardians
against wolves and other intruders. In Namibia they have even
been employed to protect livestock from cheetah attacks. Kangals
are big – around 80 centimetres (32 inches) high – and weigh
around 45 kilos (100 pounds). They are also incredibly strong and
surprisingly quick on their feet. This video claiming the breed
as the strongest in the world shows a huge Kangol pulling
a four-and-a-half ton tractor – with its mouth!

http://youtu.be/Otqe2g0MROQ

POLICE DRAMA

The feelgood video with a fantastic surprise ending

US Police officer Nick Sheppard was called out to help a dog that had managed to catch one of is hind legs in a chain link fence. A small camera attached to his hand-held radio recorded the incident as the officer is forced to carefully cut the fence in order to help the dog. When he finally managed to get the animal free, it takes off into the nearby trees. Sheppard, a self-professed "dog lover", is a little concerned and goes off in search of the runaway. What he eventually discovers, makes it worth watching the video all the way to the end.

http://youtu.be/hw4f829BPNQ

MONKEY BUSINESS

A monkey looks after three newly born puppies

What could be cuter than three newborn pups enjoying their first days on Earth? Well, how about adding a little monkey to fuss over them? If you think you can cope with an overdose of sentimentality, then take a look at this video. It shows a capuchin monkey getting to know some black and white puppies that have yet to even open their eyes. Like a doting parent, he gives them a kiss and a cuddle and deals out a lovely little pat on the head to each of them.

http://youtu.be/T9897fMrOS0

WAKEY WAKEY!

What's the best way to wake a sleeping human?

Who needs an alarm clock when you have a canine friend in the
house? This compilation shows a selection of early-riser hounds
waking their human friends. Their tactics and strategies vary
from a subtle lick on the cheek to a prod with a friendly paw to
leaping from distance with a hulking great body slam. Although
one little chap gives up and decides to snuggle up for a snooze
himself, you can only admire the bravery and persistence of these
time-wary dogs as they bring the sleepers back to reality.

http://youtu.be/CpbYBZKdi3s

PEDALLING POOCHES

The hilarious sight of Dalmatians racing on tricycles

An oldie but a goodie! This clip from a Japanese Guinness World Records show pits two Dalmatians against each other as they battle it out to be the doggy tricycle champion of the world. Both dogs show a considerable talent on two wheels, getting up quite a head of steam in the early part of the 20-metre (66-foot) race. But as their stamina is put to the test, there's a sting in the tale. The eventual winner came home in 37.59 seconds, a world record for the Fastest Time for a Dog to Cycle 20 Metres on a Tricycle.

http://youtu.be/1ZpNAl105sg

SUN ROOF SURFER

A dog hanging out a sun roof – what more do you want?

Ahhh! It's the thrill of the open road, the sensation of speed, the wind in your fur. Every dog loves to stick its head out of the window of the car, but Pilatus, a beautiful Weimaraner, gets an even better ride – he gets to put his head out of the sunroof. And clearly he loves it. Josh Hickam mounted a camera on his car roof and recorded Pilly's cheeky expressions as they went for a drive. Pilly's face is pulled this way and that, but he can't get enough of that rush of air in the face.

http://youtu.be/euplKc5Z1qU

BLESS YOU!

It's Sofie, the sneezing Shih Tzu

Say Shih Tzu quick enough a few times and it begins to sound like you are sneezing. Perhaps that is why Sofie the Shih Tzu has her sneezing impression down to a fine art. A sweet dog with an array of tricks, Sofie can stand up, roll over and do a convincing act of fixing her hair. But what sets Sofie apart from the rest of the performing dogs on YouTube is that she can sneeze on demand — and she does it in a completely adorable way.

http://youtu.be/7cJ-10gSrBg

BULLDOG IN A BOX

Big dog into little box won't go... or will it?

Bo is one brilliant bulldog. His grumpy old face alone is a hoot, but when he doggedly decides to sit in a cardboard box that is altogether too small for him, he became a viral success. Maybe Bo has convinced himself that he has a slighter figure than he really has or perhaps he just loves that box, but there is no persuading him to change. Just a little alteration to the sticky tape on the box is all he needs — even though there are plenty of suitably sized boxes available.

http://youtu.be/g8yN5fivBt8

THAT'S A BIG CAT!

A dog versus cat scenario with a twist

No dog likes having a cat in the house – least of all a big cat. Michael Jamison has had Enzo the Bengal Tiger for a while, but Whisky is a new addition to the household. The way the two new housemates react to each other is fascinating. Whisky seems to tolerate Enzo, perhaps out of respect for the pet in residence or maybe he's just never seen a cat quite that huge. But when Enzo tries it on, Whisky wastes no time in letting the tiger know who's boss. You know? I think they'll end up getting along just fine...

http://youtu.be/ld7SVrSWFdo

FLYING CARROTS

Maymo the intrepid Beagle is on a mission

Maymo's owners like to come up with ingenious ideas to entertain their Lemon Beagle. Maymo's gained some internet fame with his encounters with a battery-operated toy mouse and an inflatable shark and has proved himself a smart dog. So, how will he cope with the latest challenge – flying carrots? Maymo likes the idea of the vegetables hanging by strings from a fan. When they start to rotate, he becomes more intrigued. But Maymo is not to be underestimated. He is a intrepid dog and isn't going to be beaten by a few mid-air carrots.

http://youtu.be/gnnvely78W8

ANGRY BATH DOG

"You're not so big! I can take you!"
Watch out! Oakley is on the warpath

If Oakley was a bit bigger, he might be scary. As it is, he is just an angry little dog (according to some in the comments section, he is a Brussels Griffon). Oakley has just been given a bath and to say he is not happy about it is an understatement. He is incandescent and he has more than a few well-chosen words to aim at his owner/torturer. Unfortunately for him, the post-bath Oakley looks like, well, a scrawny rabbit and completely unthreatening. With over seven million views, this is many people's favourite video from the Talking Animals channel.

http://youtu.be/bPfZ78m3xZo

EMPTY POOL BLUES

No water in the pool? These puppies just can't believe it!

Cute puppy time again – and this time there are 10 of them (I think – they don't stay still for long!). These adorable Golden Retriever puppies are just five weeks old, but they are old enough to know when something just isn't right. The morning play in the paddling pool that they have come to think of as a basic puppy right hasn't happened... there's no water in the pool! What is there for a gang of young pups to do about it – except wander around in a disbelieving fashion and get very angry and slightly sad.

http://youtu.be/3ZqPaohVjmw

CLYDE WANTS A KITTY

**Clyde has been promised a new friend,
but will he get what he wished for?**

Canadian actor/comedian Andrew Grantham, who brought us
Clark, the dog who was teased to torment about the meat treats
in the fridge, introduces us to another canine chum, Clyde. This
excitable pup is expecting news about the new friend his owner
has been to the pet shop to collect. Clyde is hoping for a kitten! He
really, really wants a kitten friend. So how does he react when he's
told of all the other appealing creatures available at the shop? Is
he excited about the prospect of a snake to play with? Or jumping
at the idea of a guinea pig pal? Nope. Clyde just wants a kitty...

http://youtu.be/kl4yoXyb1_M

PUPPY LOVE

Harvey and Harmony – a match made in doggy heaven

It's a modern day love story... Harvey and Harmony meet at speed dating, go on a first date to the cinema, take yoga class together, visit the museum (and steal a rather large dinosaur bone), spend some together time on a sunny day picnic and get romantic in the back of a car! But when Harvey's owner answers a ring on the doorbell, the old romantic has some explaining to do! It's just an promo video for the power of television advertising, but why let that get in the way of a good old romantic yarn?

http://youtu.be/Ga7eVrqTrAw

NO SLEEPING ON THE JOB

He might be dog-tired, but this puppy is determined to see the job through...

"I must stay awake... I must stay awake." Looking after a tiny baby can be a tiring task, but this little puppy has a self-appointed job and he is determined to stick to it. As the baby quietly slumbers, the poor puppy stands guard despite his eyes becoming ever heavier and his head beginning to droop. He fights off the sleep again and again until he's given permission to go off duty and have a well-earned nap. If you think this is sweet, just wait until you see what happens next...

http://y2u.be/xuyCdgpa5sY

MAGIC MEAT

Heads up! It's a levitating sausage

More fun and games from supreme dog teaser Jose Ahonen. This time the magician and mentalist explores (more for fun than for science) how dogs react to a levitating hot dog sausage. If there is anything that will test a pooch's mental capacities, it is a floating meat treat. Jose manages to magically suspend a wiener (an American hot dog sausage) in mid-air just out of reach of the hungry hounds. Of course, some of them have a good attempt at snapping it up straight away, but more fun are those that are bewitched, bemused or, best of all, totally freaked by the experiment.

http://youtu.be/9Db6JZHh0SA

DEAR DIARY

The innermost thoughts of the saddest of dogs

"Dear diary, it occurred to me today that my dearest human has never sniffed my backside." The sad dog diary delves into the psyche of some deep thinking dogs and reveals their innermost thoughts. Some of these might be unpalatable and even a little obscene to the human ear, but hey, it's a dog's life. So feast your eyes on a selection of world weary canines and chuckle away to their thoughts on just why we collect their poo in plastic bags and exactly what kind of deal they think they are sealing when they shake hands.

http://youtu.be/Xw1C5T-fH2Y

DEAD CAT BOUNCE

Give this moggy an Oscar, unless I don't catch him first!

Are we running a little short on dog versus cat videos? "Yes!"
calls a chorus of hounds up and down the country. So let's try
to straighten that score with a scene just out of Tom and Jerry.
There's a cat motionless, on its back in the middle of the road.
What is anyone supposed to think? The poor creature must have
come to a sorry end. It has gone to the great cat home
in the sky. And here's a sympathetic dog, showing concern
for a fellow creature. So he goes to check on the health
of the kitty and gets the surprise of his life...

http://youtu.be/xY672bb9qc4

CUTEST CHECK -UP

Uncomplaining Bull Terrier undergoes toddler vet act

Neckar is one special dog. He doesn't wail, wriggle or bark when faced with a veterinary check-up. He does, however, have the cutest vet ever. Manuel Ruiz Villarreal filmed this video of his daughter, Noa, playing doctor with the family's Bull Terrier. The toddler performs a thorough check-up. She gives Neckar his shots, then checks both his ears and finally makes sure everything is in working order with a once-over with her plastic stethoscope. And all the time, Neckar, the most patient dog patient in the world sits there without a murmur.

http://youtu.be/hWcEljkLsVo

A SHAGGY DOG STORY

The Fairy Tale of the Airline Lost and Found Dog

Like Peter Pan said, you just have to believe. So try to believe in
this ad from Dutch airline KLM. You'll meet Sherlock, a beautiful
Beagle who works with the airline's lost and found team. Sherlock
is the epitome of caring service — he's not interested in drugs,
contraband or illegal foodstuffs; Sherlock tracks down owners of
lost phones and other cherished posessions left on the plane and
returns them as the owners queue to leave the airport. He really is
a darling. Does Sherlock really exist? Well, you just have to believe.

http://y2u.be/NK-T_t166TY

FRITZ LEARNS TO CATCH

The chronicle of a dog who drops everything thrown for him

Some people just can't catch. They lack the necessary hand-eye co-ordination. So why should it be funny when a dog proves as ineffectual at catching? No reason. But it really is. Here's a compilation of poor Fritz's quest to learn how to catch food. He is gently lobbed every foodstuff a dog might desire: steak, a strawberry, a chimichanga, a meatball – and drops the lot. But Fritz is nothing if not committed to the task. And who wouldn't stand and applaud when he finally takes that flying chip clean out of the air – almost.

http://y2u.be/6w2UxDdhZPk

SEALED WITH A KISS

It came from the sea... in search of a cuddle

Those nature programmes on TV would have you believe that the natural world is a cut-throat business where species face off with species on every corner. OK. You know where this is going... Elise Frebourg was on the beach with friends when he captured a rare and completely adorable incident. For no apparent reason, a seal climbs out of the water onto the beach. He waddles up to a resting Labrador and plonks himself down on it. Of course, this isn't a ghastly ambush, but a charming attempt by the seal to snuggle up to the dog for some cuddles. Awwww!

http://youtu.be/wqnmuAWxleQ

OVERCOME WITH EMOTION

A happy reunion is just too much for this Schnauzer

Casey, the family Schnauzer, had missed Rebecca. She had been away for two years and that's an awful long time in dog years. So when Rebecca finally shows up, poor Casey is pretty happy to see her. Now, many dogs wiggle, squeal and leap on such occasions, but Casey takes the biscuit. After some serious yelping he is quite literally overcome with joy. A later video called *#CaseyTheDog | a sequel* shows what happened next time Rebecca returned from a long trip. Anyone else wondering if she just goes away because she loves the attention?

http://youtu.be/rp03AorAWLY

GO! BWAH!

A small girl with a bigger dog on a lead... uh oh!

At two seconds long, this is definitely the shortest video in the book. But it is also quite possible the funniest or even the most hilarious two seconds on the net. It's just a small child with a dog on a leash, but it is pure comedy gold. Others on YouTube have remixed it and put it to music, but when the original is this good it's difficult to improve on it. Unless... you are the kind of person who can't stop laughing at someone falling over. In that case some kind soul has compiled a feature-length version in *Go Bwah 10 Minute Repeat*.

http://youtu.be/dgKGixi8bp8

WANNABE CELEBRITY DOG

Another step to fame for Crusoe the Dachshund

According to his very own website, Crusoe the Dachsund is "The wiener dog who thinks he's more of a celebrity than he really is (for now)". Well, Crusoe is not doing too badly at the celebrity game. He has 20,000 subscribers to his channel, he's done TV around the world and has his own T-shirt, book and calendar store. What's more, he has quite possibly the most entertaining 15 seconds on the internet as he and his brother, Oakley, play cops and robbers. If you like this, there is a Part 2 and another video where the brothers play firefighters. Unmissable.

http://youtu.be/znM9YD2J3Cw

COOKING WITH DOG

**A canine-assisted Japanese cookery show?
You better believe it!**

Don't worry. *Cooking with Dog* is not some horrific recipe show
in which dogs are cooked. It is, however, quite bizarre. This
YouTube cooking show that has nearly a million subscribers
features a canine host Francis and an anonymous Japanese
chef. While the chef cooks a variety of popular Japanese dishes,
Francis calmly sits next to her and narrates the recipes step-
by-step in his amusing French-tinged English. The clip linked
here is a trailer for the show and gives you a taster for the
show in case you want to create some tasty meals.

http://youtu.be/hUfc_3OErYw

THE PUG HEAD TILT

Three Pugs fail their synchronized head swivel audition

These Pugs — Mabel, Minnie and Max — won the internet in 2015 with their marvellous head-tilting performance. Now, experts can explain until they're blue in the face that this is just animal behaviour, the dogs putting their ears in the most effective position possible. But we prefer to believe that the three Ms just haven't rehearsed their choreography and furrowed brow expressions enough. And, all discipline breaks down when their human friend asks if they want to go to the ball park. You can almost hear the remaining pug crying, "Call yourself professionals?".

http://youtu.be/9uuqXXT7VYo

PASTA LA VISTA, BABY

An eating race that's over almost as soon as it's begun

Competitive eating is all over YouTube. Everywhere you look,
Joey Chestnut and Kobayashi are pigging out like you wouldn't
believe. So it was only a matter of time before the pooches got
in on the act. A Golden Retriever and a German Shepherd each
square up to a huge bowl of spaghetti. When it comes to wolfing
it down in double-quick time, who's your money on? Here's a
clue — one of them goes at it like a truck driver, devouring
the whole lot in under four seconds, while the other savours
his meal, taking nearly three minutes.

http://y2u.be/dYTSS14SFY0

STUFF ON SCOUT'S HEAD

The amazing balancing rescue Pit bull

A Pit bull named Scout became the first canine hero of the short blog site Tumblr. His owner, on a mission to show that not all Pit bulls were snarling psychopaths, posted a series of photos of Scout. It became apparent that Scout, a rescued dog who was neglected, starved and abused, had an uncanny ability to balance anything on his head. Whether it's a sombrero or a single strawberry or a baseball, he not only manages to remain still, but looks utterly adorable at the same time. This is YouTube's tribute to the fabulous dog's posts.

http://youtu.be/NzUDKcp5C_8

BARKING BACK-CHAT

A hilarious "argument" ensues when a Husky answers back

"So my husky stole my dad's potato skins off his plate. This was the ensuing argument." This Husky sure has some guts. When Dad starts on him, shouting, "You stay out of my stuff! That's mine!", the Husky has a few words (or whimpers) to say under his breath. Unfortunately, Dad is not prepared to let it lie; it's hard to tell whether he is joking or not when he treats the mutt like an errant teenager. But what develops is absolutely hilarious — an argument between man and animal in which the pooch gives as good as he gets.

http://youtu.be/ZDhK4Lrh7OA

ANYONE FOR TENNIS?

Georges the tennis-loving dog

Every dog loves a tennis ball. It is usually a slobbered-over, ragged ball, not the new ones that Georges here is mesmerized by. There's tennis on the television – the Australian Open in this case – and Golden Retriever Georges is ready. He excitedly leaps up and down, playing every point – stopping only briefly for a rest at the end of a rally. Apparently, he loves watching any sport, but tennis is his favourite. Nevertheless, the best moment is when the camera pans to Georges's canine friend whose blank look says, "What on earth is he on?".

http://youtu.be/kZm6RwukFCc

SQUAD CAR TRAINED

Is this the smartest dog on the force?

There are quite a few good guard or police dog training videos available to view on YouTube. Many of them, like this clip, feature the work of dogs in the fabulously named K9 SWAT Units in the USA. Usually they involve the German Shepherd performing diligent and ruthless jaw work in apprehending criminals, but this law enforcement hound has another string to his bow. He can open the squad car door, get in and shut the door – on his own. While you watch, have a thought for the officer who says, "Don't get me on YouTube" – it's been viewed nearly two million times!

http://youtu.be/ip7sz6Z8obE

CHARLIE PUTS IT RIGHT

A guilty dog does his best to make amends

Charlie the Beagle really found himself in the dog house when he stole baby Laura's toys. When Charlie hot foots it from the cot with her favourite soft mobile, Laura sounds off in the only way she knows. There's no hiding the crime, so Charlie decides to make amends. Soon the contrite canine is showering her with gifts from around the house, including soft dolls, a tennis ball, and even a PlayStation controller. In no time, poor Laura is buried under a pile of toys, but it seems to do the trick; she stops crying.

http://youtu.be/eV8k2cpAptU

POSING POOCH PRANK

Mum freaks out to a fake dog in the house

Jimmy O'Brien's mum is scared to death of his brother's German Shepherd. That might seem fair enough, many people have a fear of dogs. This particular dog, however, is completely harmless. It is a fake dog. Despite having a real dog in the house, Jimmy bought his little bro a pretty passable life-sized stuffed dog. It isn't scary, actually it's pretty cute, but it proved perfect for scaring the wits out of their poor mother. Every time she happens across the furry fake around the house, she lets out a hilarious scream of surprise.

http://youtu.be/eaxr-YoGcKo

RAIDERS OF THE LOST BARK

A puppy Indy is the star of this brilliant film remake

Boxer puppy Indy is perfect in the Harrison Ford role in the remake of this great film. In the trademark hat, he is the star of this five-minute film *Indiana Bones – Raiders of the Lost Bark*. It's a real hoot as it recreates the film's great stunts, including Indy using his whip to swing across a gap, having to rescue his hat from under a closing door and escaping a giant rolling boulder. And, of course, all the time he has to escape the evil Nazis – played here by kittens! A masterpiece.

http://y2u.be/7ydBgdL5R08

PARKOUR DOG

Meet TreT – the dog with some awesome free running moves

If TreT was a human, he'd be running around in baggy trousers and skate shoes. As it is, the five-year-old American Staffordshire Terrier has to make do with a cool black harness as he pulls off his pretty cool parkour moves. When he goes for walkies, the dog known to his fans as Parkour Dog from Ukraine isn't happy with a jog around the park. TreT has been trained in the fine art of hardcore urban manoeuvring and this trailer for his many popular videos shows him in glorious action; leaping railings, climbing walls and jumping from ledge to ledge.

http://youtu.be/nBtJVrx4Mzs

DOG VS. BALLOONS

Simon is more than a match for a room full of balloons

Over 30 million people have watched this clip. It is one of the
most popular videos in this book and yet it lasts only a minute,
is not particularly cute and doesn't even feature a puppy. Simon
the Terrier loves popping balloons. Indeed, he is the Guinness
record holder for balloon popping and clearly has a passion for
his hobby. Let loose in a room with 74 balloons on a rug,
he is a master at work; picking off the outer ring, moving
quickly on if one doesn't pop easily and keeping his control
(apart from one moment of overexcitement). In just
57 seconds, Simon's work is done. What a pro!

http://youtu.be/CoiFGva_JoY

THE GREAT ESCAPE

"Houdini" Beagle stars in fence-busting thriller

"I'm going over the fence, Chalky. See you on the outside."
OK, it is not exactly *The Great Escape*, but this pooch's break for
freedom is mighty impressive. The owners set up the camera
because they couldn't work out how their Beagle was escaping
from his cage. This video explains it all. The ingenious hound
had worked out how to scale the fence that is 1.8 metres
6 feet) high and then squeeze himself through the rickety roof.
Just watch the touching concern of his fellow prisoners as
our Houdini Beagle takes his brave leap for freedom.

http://youtu.be/MLssW7Iyzxw

A DOG WITH BOUNCE

Chago gets some serious air on the trampoline

It's a Boxer on a trampoline. That's it, folks. But you'll still love it. The caption calls Chago the world's most loved Boxer – and they have a point. The clip of the happy-go-lucky hound getting some decent air on the trampoline has been viewed over three million times on YouTube and shared 27 million times on Facebook! There is obviously something life-affirming and cheery about the way Chago is just so happy bouncing away. And he's not even a puppy. Perhaps they could make it an Olympic event?

http://youtu.be/HIy0vuXPG-M

DOG ON WIRE

Introducing Ozzy, the amazing tightrope walking dog

The *Daily Mail* rather amusingly called Osbert Humperdinck
Pumpernickle, "the collie who never wobbles". Ozzy (as he is
always known) is actually a Border Collie and Kelpie cross, but the
other part is accurate for he is the world's best canine tightrope
walker. Ozzy's parents were sheepdogs, but the young dog obviously
had ambitions to run away to the circus. He has developed an
amazing sense of balance as demonstrated in this slacklining
(balancing on a loosely hung rope) video. Elsewhere on YouTube
you can see more of his balancing acts, including his
Guinness World Record-breaking tightrope walk.

http://youtu.be/d4afy5q2cSM

ON YOUR BIKE

The bicycle guard dog who hops on for a ride

Here is yet another nomination for Best Dog in the World Ever.
The canine in question is a Golden Retriever in China. Not only
does he guard the bicycle while the rider pops into the shop;
when the owner shows up, he climbs aboard the rack on the
bike. Now watch carefully and you'll notice his owner waits for
the dog to bark that he is safely aboard before peddling away.
Now that is super cool! The dog has become such a
celebrity that a campaign has begun to help buy
a more comfortable seat for the loyal mutt.

http://youtu.be/z1SubT8ldno